In the Days of the D

Pterosaur's Long Flig

Story by Hugh Price

Illustrations by Ben Spiby

Long, long ago,
two pterosaurs had a nest
at the top of a big cliff.

There were four baby pterosaurs
in the nest.
They had come out of their eggs
a week ago.
Now they were always hungry.

Sometimes the mother pterosaur
flew away to get food for the babies.
Sometimes the father pterosaur went.

One warm morning,
the father pterosaur
took off from the top of the cliff
to look for food.

He put out his wings,
ran along the cliff top,
and jumped.

He went up and up in the warm air.

Way down on the ground
he saw a herd of triceratops
eating the trees.

The triceratops had great big legs
and great big heads
and great big horns.

This was no place for a pterosaur.
The father pterosaur flew on.

When he looked down again,
he saw Tyrannosaurus rex,
who was walking along
looking for food.

Tyrannosaurus rex
was **enormous**.

This was no place
for a pterosaur.

The father pterosaur flew over a river.
He came flying down
to look for fish,
but he saw some crocodiles.
He flew up again.

This was no place for a pterosaur!

Back at the nest the baby pterosaurs
were getting **very** hungry.

Then the father pterosaur came to a lake.
He flew over it
and looked down into the water.

He saw lots of fish.
They were swimming past a big log.

Yes!
This was the place for a pterosaur!

He flew down to the lake,
opened his jaws,
and filled them with fish, but...

the log opened **its** jaws, too.
The log was a hungry crocodile!

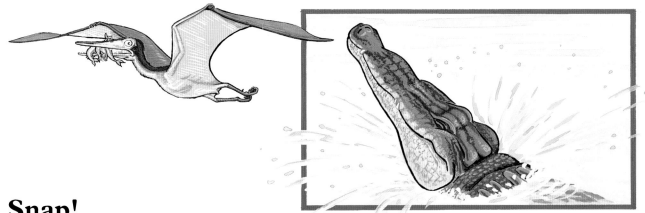

Snap!
The father pterosaur flew up again,
just in time.

Away he went,
all the way back to the nest,
where the four hungry little pterosaurs
were all **very** pleased
to see him.

16